Splen

MW01254437

Jude Neale

SPM Publications

London

SPM Publications
Unit 136, 113-115 George Lane, South Woodford,
London E18 1AB, United Kingdom
www.spmpublications.com

First published in Great Britain by SPM Publications – an imprint of
Sentinel Writing & Publishing Company in April 2017.

ISBN 978-0-9935035-5-9

Sentinel Writing & Publishing Company is a division of SPM Publications
Ltd.

Set in Garamond 9 – 16 points.
Cover photo: 'Wolf Moon' ©2017 Jim Crotty www.jimcrotty.com

To Audrey,
Paulie, Soph, James,
Marion and Steve
with love

Acknowledgements

Many people have helped birth this book. From conception to completion, I have been helped by those familiar with the intimate language of poetry.

Thanks go to Elaine Taylor, Lidia Patriasz and Paul Hooson for reading each poem, and contributing valuable and constructive criticism. Your enthusiasm and keen eye has been invaluable.

Gratitude to Audrey Grescoe for her absolutely clear and careful editing. Hours of thought and consideration went into this venture. She helped me to recognize when a spade is simply a spade!

I would also like to thank Pulp Literature for choosing many of these poems for their shortlists over the years. Their enthusiastic support has been deeply appreciated.

Many thanks to my family, Katie, Geoff and Jeremy, for being the grist for my mill. I realize how much of our lives are told through these poems, and how invasive this must have seemed at times.

Finally, I would like to thank Bonnie Nish and Candice James for their unflagging encouragement, over many years. They have booked me for many readings and collaborated on projects that enriched both my writing and my personal life.

Contents

Foreword

This collection, ***Splendid in its Silence***, tells of need and longing, to offer love and be loved, and finally set free. It speaks of daughters and sons, mothers and fathers, and the unbreakable bond of a lover and friend.

For it is true that words are the tools that lift fleeting moments to permanence, and clarity from confusion.

Each poem shows an imagistic portrait to be looked at through the lens of beauty and the troubling impermanence of time.

I hope that you, the reader, will dip into each poem with a sense of renewal and light.

Jude Neale

Jude Neale has written:

The Perfect Word Collapses
Only the Fallen Can See
A Quiet Coming of Light
Splendid in its Silence
Line by Line, Neale/Nish

CDs:

Places Beyond
Wild Rose Suite
Tonight
Home to stay

SPLENDID IN ITS SILENCE

And still within a summer's night
A something so transporting bright
I clap my hands to see,

Then veil my too inspecting face
Lest such a subtle, shimmering grace
Flutter too far for me-

Emily Dickinson
from *'A something in a summer's Day'*

Splendid in its Silence

Only when she's quiet and doesn't speak
can she hear his breath
slide from parted lips.

I want to kiss you
the way I used to,
pressed against your chest.

I'm afraid to steal what is not mine.

Take bread away from me if you wish,
I'm full of yesterday's laughter.
The spin of your voice,
the light touch of your hand on mine.

You are my reason for fullness.

I groan with my need to carry you
in marsh and shadow,
you comfort me.

My love, splendid in its silence

splits me in two.

Love Brag Poem

Yah. I know how to please.

I am a celestial choir
and sing my proud anthem
with one mighty moan.

I show the boys
a black and white photo
of my silky thigh bones -
and who is to blame?

I'm their golden goddess of pleasure

and am graced by fine hands
and a musk scented stride.

It's more than rumour
that brings them

to my ripe acres of heat

I lie each of them down
awake and asleep

where they give way
like ships' timber

and howl back at me

Queen of the Boudoir
waker of dreams

I'm here to tell all

it's just what it
just what it
just what it

seems.

Relief of Touch

The cool relief of touch.
A legacy from an earlier time,
when pushing was the first thing
we knew.
Blood and bone
bound my life to yours,

oh daughter,
of fathomless conception.

The Blanket

Sometimes you just strike it rich.

Perhaps it's the sunlight

squares on the cream
blanket you wore

as your life seeped into the tips of your fingers,

and he held them tightly to the tune of *Lily Marlene*.

He watched your portcullis mouth
trap air redolent with the need
for him planted
before his first breath.

The white fury of his gratefulness
choked the jasmine bells of your fear.

He stank of a sort of filial kindness -

the inevitable loneliness marked
by your merciless, meandering passing.

Blue Heron

Maple leaves wave, yellow spades
unwilling to give up the light.

A blue heron, wings arching
crests the tree,

pewter threaded through china gold.

Her leaden shadow spreads
across the landscape

huddled from my watery view.

Wild Berry

In memory of Mary Greener Thompson

She once followed bear scat
to find the low-bush blueberries hidden

high above the wide emerald mouth
of the North Thompson river.

She was still and unguarded -

and let the swarm of blackflies crawl
in her ears,
down the back of her neck.

She knelt beside the fruit
and imagined
a life in the city -

where no one would care
about the wild berries

she had dropped like gold coins
into the empty tin pail.

****

Summer nights in Vancouver
she'd stroll with her friends
down *Granville Street*

where she let her cigarette burn down
to ash in the corner of her red mouth

It was the ways of the bad girls

who painted their faces
and tinted their finger-waved hair
that she memorized.

She wanted to sing love songs
to strangers

who'd mistake
her voice for the river

and her small courage for faith

that was held in the grace
of church basement Bingo

and the transparent fruit jelly
she plucked from the bushes like beads.

****

The dragonfly hovers and settles
onto her raven haired beauty.

It flickers iridescent blue green wings
a peacock's wondrous eye

of colour and light.

She picks in the shiver of morning
when the black rooted cliffs

shift from shadow to blue.

The berries roll into the bucket
purple mementos

to be pressed
against tongue against teeth

in the heavy white winter
when colour is the only thing

she wants to believe.

Eighty-five Green Candles

Birthday preparations

I turn her alabaster back towards
the fancy hotel's shower,

gently stroke

her filth
covered bum
with my bare hands.

How do I erase my cool malice
that I carry from *Barbie*, *Leave it to Beaver*

and the transformative blessing
of being Shirl's girl?

Now she steals my love by omission -

fashions it from rolls of pillowy soft
double-strength toilet paper,

that she carefully unrolls like dough
onto the bathroom's white floor.

Let me dry you with ten weeping towels
piled in the sink. You look away in shame,

look away.

Thank you

for teaching me how to forgive
your frailties and flesh eating loss.

This ancient act of bathing
sucks at my breasts -

call me your mother,
call me your daughter,

Call me your own.

Darling Boy

He cuts a sabered swathe
through my stale air

inhabits the room of youth

I stand aside measuring
the day with the tick of silence

while he flings fortune into the wake
of my comfortable lassitude

He changes brass to gold
in the heat of his tensile beginnings

The Blue Danube Moon

We sit on the porch
talk in grey whispers
unsure of the night

You kiss my surprised lips
though they are faded with disuse

A change
in the weather
would be all
it would take

to ring the blue Danube moon
sitting on the broken stone wall

Runs like Kite String

Don't bother to be honest, emptying
your need for confession into my ear

I don't want to be laden with the words
soaked in the piety of your complaint

My silent dissatisfaction with forgiveness
is the crime that runs like kite-string

through the well-oiled door of my heart

Post Op

I fantasize

what it would feel like
to be you,

if you were you.

I know this is a bad time to mention it,

but

I want to rise
singing anthems

rather than pace
this two o'clock place

on the carpet

never trusting

the right time
to say:

Baby, let me rip off your bruised skin,

and shine like a silverfish
over our bloodletting loss.

Crack this silence that throws
us both on the ropes.

What can I do
with my kindle of heat?

Your white marble thighs slides
between our blue floral sheets.

And I know I can't look.

I might wish for more.

We're two gypsy dancers
in a room with no floors.

I hold your loss like an oyster

where the grit is your sadness
and my ache is your pearl.

I never once asked you
to lie, naked with shame.

I am to blame, love. I am to blame.

Pink

pink spells
pink grapefruit pink

camellias pink tongues

pink lipstick pink
tears pink puddle
pink knuckles pink

song pink dreams
pink throat pink
whispers pink want

pink heart pink
shudders pink echo
pink sex pink

breast pink sleep
pink breath pink

longing pink yes

pink kiss pink
love pink forever
pink endings pink

birdsong pink sky

Lost and Found

This clutch of cold
snowy pills transform me

from a rock, a feather
to a mere stencil of bone.

My witless ghost is mirrored
in the unwashed appliances
spacing my wet words.

They make me choke
on satellite whispers

when I'm held hush
in small measure
for you.

My grief is soaking the weary blue gown
I wear to this ham handed ball
where I only dance with the devil
who faked he could save me

from my quiet ruin.

If I had a pyrite bed,
I would gather the hard shimmer of moons
falling into blackness of the night before
and lapse into the brave singular ending
beginning with,

this is me, my little daughter

this is me.

Emptiness in the Garden

Your sheets are pulled back
to reveal the small impression

you left for me to guard.

Your head laid here full
of big dreams.

I walk with disbelief around the path
that I have worn so thick
with your parting

Towels capture your scent
the way moss fills chinks
of emptiness in the garden

Passing

His smile, a half-moon set in stone
filled that evening,

and I knew that death
was no antidote
for life.

He had chosen this path
inflamed with rage.

I was unmoored

on the bordered shore
floating like a Chinese paper lantern

consumed.

The Disappearance

Her eyes were hazel, two agates
watched my every move.

Stroke
listen to her breathing quiet.

I whispered into her ear
tender words of mercy and release.

Stroke.

We lay quiet touching
this cold iceberg loss
unable to hide our love.

It hung like balloons over
the striped Mexican blanket.

The room gave up light
when she lay down
to sleep,

to dream of tall meadow grass
with me and the sun
instead of this useless ache I hold.

Stroke. Remember
there is no black hole but forgetting

and nothing more can be claimed
with my hot tears.

Treasures Found

I'm hungry for beach glass

to gather, polish and make gifts for our night.
Their fire will burn the unending questions

of *'where do I come from* or *how do I go?'*

One thing's for certain,
this sky holds its secrets,
like a bowl of blood oranges
holds the rust of the day.
.

Maybe I gleam more now
since you've touched me,

for I open before you and say

hold me
like this
till I feel my skin settle.

You smoky eyed figment of uncommon bliss.

The Bracelet

I cried years
for your leaving

even practised my cool-palmed benediction
over your glory
opening like a yellow narcissus

but you vanished before I could tell you

to raise the white flag if you fell
over and over

into someone else's movie
where you were never the lead

you wheeled past me
like a flat stone

over a frozen backed pond

I can't find my way back home without you
and call out your name

Katie

it falls like cool water
over my third degree burns

summer evenings when you were 10
we'd lie spread-eagled on the trampoline

watching for Cassiopeia
with her clutch of bowed moons

this slim copper bracelet
you gave me

is where you settle
deep in my thoughts.

and I feel the click of the catch
in my throat
as I slide the turquoise beads
back to the beginning
to be joined   once again

Small Gifts

Once my small dimpled fingers
plucked button-hole daisies and weeds

from the backyard lawn,

before we visited my mother
at the *Nanaimo General* hospital.

Dad scrubbed my face pink,
with the rough flannel cloth

so that she would know
someone still had control
over my solemn young life.

We stood together,
Mum's motherless children

under the gaze of her second floor window.

I blew three kisses as loud as I could,

and hoped to penetrate
the insoluble view

of brick and curtained rooms

with my milky clutch of yellow dandelions.

Shipwrecked

I'm shipwrecked by your words,

drowned
by their burden.

What use is my silence
that changes confusion to regret?

I'm not prepared
for the questions
you lob at me.

I won't open my clenched eyes for you.

Your accusations can't penetrate
my cool Novocain numbness,

for I'm perfectly at peace
inside my steel affability.

Small Lives

We lie by the fire,
arms, legs, my wet hair
and sleet burned skin.

I watch the Balinese shadows,
climb the wall.

As I dress,
your hand catches
my thin gold chain, scatters blood
coloured beads
across the hearth,

small lives, separating.

On my way home,
the moon no longer floats
but riffles like gauze
while a ring burns round it.

The muddy path is luminous
like the eyes of a fortune teller.

Frogs embed in the banks of the river.

I cross the bridge
skip over each fault,

and pull my mantle of secrets
across my emerald eyes.

His disappointment waits

like smoke
in a smokeless room.

My bloodied hands
press the latch,

Lady Macbeth before the fall.

Not Just Another Fish Story

In homage to Patrick Lane
Thanks to Mark Doty for the image of mackerel

The rude dust once snaked under your cap
when you were a boy

and you didn't dither or hang back

just left a question mark
in those railings of boned sky
you called home.

Now you gaze with fresh gratitude
at the small flicks of summer moths
as they plunder the heavy browed night.

Dig in the earth
to look for your voice
and pull out a word

alive

with the stasis of mackerel
and the delicious hard bite

of this one

luminescent moment
caught in relief.

Nana's Hat

Hat Trick

I hummed   like the river
in the heat of the morning

when breezes ran low
        against banks
drawn with mud.

I fluttered with green
breath   and tended
no master,

in the shelter of   deer fern's
unfurled   early   buds.

But   decades   close doors
on   linear thinking

and I know   living
is final - and dust
is just   dust.

To see   all the   sunsets
and   know
their full meaning,

is the one thing   a skeptic
like me   can believe.

I once   hoped for
      an anthem   of answers
on this flat   open   highway
where I wept   and   I loved.

Now I feel
the angry   flick   of a feather
curled   under   the   brim

of the fine velvet hat
that   Nana   wore

-when she stepped
onto   the one penny gum
with her   best   shoes
            on Granville Street.

Her ghost   of a frown
forever   netted
by the *Pulice brothers*

in the black and white photo
I plucked   from   the box.

She stared   straight ahead
through   seventy years

at my   vagrant   curiosity.

Cartoon Our Grief

The last heart beat breaks
the silence
spun of held breath and wishes
that press between our crossed fingers
We become business-like
dabbing eyes with hard balls of tissue
Red roses and get-well cards
cartoon our grief
I carefully tuck back the hair sticking
to your already cooling cheek.
Tell myself that endings
leave no mementos
of a life well lived.

What You Know You Cannot Keep

It is that time just before a breaking

The dark that exposes light
or the pain before pleasure

that moment when you hold your breath
to hear your own heart beat

There is so little that you know
and what you know
you cannot keep

The old cat plays with a loose thread

You see yourself scowl
in a cowgirl costume

and try to remember
how this smile

so deeply worn
was put there

Feathers Gathered, Feathers Lost

Jewish Community Centre
Thoughts after an exhibition

We speak them
into shadowed lives

They balloon our dry throats
with malice and the recognizable
gossip of our station and design

These words drift like pollen
over sleepy blank tongues
eager for a bitter taste
to inform them
of the hard rub of someone else's
slim bag of misery

We ask ourselves
who are we to paint you
with such sticky tar
casting stones
at your blind innocence

Now we try to gather
back the words
that have stained
your spotless name

The wind lifts
the feathered flutter
of these secrets and lies
and it blows them clean
away from our
undeserving eyes

We *promise*
    we're *sorry*

and won't whisper
won't   *whisper*   again
the mean truths
that held your face
to the night

Is This Your Final Answer?

I hear her time smudged steps

and imagine my once swan throated mother
leaning on the bedroom window sill

trapping my dad
with a *Moscow Square* kiss

tossed
randomly from her lips to his.

But that was before
her skin turned to paper
threaded with aubergine veins.

Today I should've ridden the high seas
on the overcrowded ferry

to deposit my husk of a mother
back at her home
for dementia.

But once again
I become a child

biting my nails

feeding my anger
with my own skin.

She picks at my time
with her manicured nails.

I lock my boredom
into the bathroom
where I sulkily squeeze
out a small borax of tears.

Mother is the woman
I never could love,

even though restlessly

she carried me and my brother
for six whirling months

between her willowy thighs.

Now she sticks her tongue out
at strangers, snidely comments

on the size of
bellies or butts.

I become the hairy lipped
gym teacher
teaching her kegels

during the flood on the couch

where she plays solitaire
and wins every game.

Hours drain within this quicksand
of stand and deliver.

I can't feed her enough of myself.

I tuck my guilt around her

with a sleeping pill, hoping
this will tip her away
from our severed bond.

Mother, I am lost   to you,
even when you implore me

naked at 7:00 a.m.

with your two favourite questions:

What is next?

What
is
next?

Black Fish Out of Time

I have done it again.

Torn off your clothes,
to find underneath
your penchant for kneeling.

You come to me broken,
unable to open your wings.

You dissolved on my carpet
to become a black fish out of time

grasping the hook, I could tell
you never intended to let go

of the invisible thread leading
to death's imponderable loneliness

Foreign Ways

I like to know that your smile
will run like water over my eyes.
That I will laugh
at just the right word
you toss at my fumbling hands.
I wait for the moment
when I open my body
to the scorch of your breath.
An offering
of forgiveness
for my foreign ways.

Dress Up

In the cage of the car at 5:45
I flick my forked tongue against you
and spit back your words

They explode from my lips
into your plugged ears

You cannot take from me
the steel I found
that winter

when I was but a whisper
in my grandfather's throat

I have seen both sides of the cloth
where obsidian meets sky

I shall straighten my skirt
and wear a tropical garden
round my waist

hiding my rage

at the expressive arts party at six

Black Patent Shoes

I sit in front of the choir stall,
an edgy soprano
myopically ready
to send reedy notes
of blessing to my neighbours
bent in prayer.

Light filters through,
a dusty spotlight to the infinite.

The child strokes her mother's shoulder,
flowery head waits for the call of her name.

Her eyes are wide with curiosity

at the blessing of water to skin.

Belief and purity
mix in this room,

under the shaft of light
of the quivering candle.

Shadows dance
on the child's elation
from the liturgy

and her new patent shoes.

Midsummer Bewilders the Dog Star

Poised
in the slanted light of evening
midsummer bewilders the Dog Star

A lullaby flies low
over the trees
invokes the circular calm
of the indigo skies

Melt the edges of my fatigue
before my wishing
my praying
my negotiating eyes

A Body of Lies

no

I will never leave
this nest we have made

from the snatches of yellow daffodils
you gave me

when I thought
only roses

would do. I tied a ribbon round

my neck
petal soft

a noose
for my gladness

but

thank you anyway

for pointing it out
that my substance isn't ghostly
or a mere possibility

it's the one truth

of my transmuted body
that doesn't tell lies

Newly Born

To Aria and Ursula

Sing Aria into breath.

A sea star she fastens
onto my silk strands of gladness

silk strands, make rope, *mio cara.*

I will build a swing for you to fly
into my arms and back to the tree.

Rope we have gathered between us
strong like our bond

and light as the delicate beating
of your hummingbird heart.

How to Pin Down a Fevered River

It's the smell of oil paints she carried
down to the rocks to pin down a fevered river.

The deep Prussian skies
of summer we breathed her in,

sap green and happy.
She made my life shimmer,

a jar of bubbles,
transfused by the sun.

Do I Feed It or Starve It?

This thirst for explosives
depths of bottle green ocean

My cool hand only
vaguely waves in the right direction
while you crash through the world
screaming why

I hand you words like soap
to eradicate the traces
of the fledgling man of tomorrow

Then cross my fingers
And hope that our cable is strong

So you can dive and soar
upward with flames

while I implode with held breath

My Cold Sorrow

Like Dorothy,
in that terrible field of poppies -

let me fall
asleep at last.

Undefended,
palms turned up
to the ceiling.

Muffled night
hear my cries.

Suck at my pain,
taste the black juice

of my cold sorrow.

The Thief

the red startle of duct tape
on the edge of your date book

is your way of pissing

on perfection

when broken things claim you
like rats from a sewer

you bind them to you
with stolen orange prayer flags
to keep them

from floating away

with the dish and the spoon
til the little dog laughed

but your lenses are missing
and your suitcase is full

of clown noses, shady hollows
that won't be broken or fixed

beat the drum softly
with the secret code
of the thief

then we'll all follow you

with a skip
drag
and sing

Au Jus

Lorna Crozier's 'Compendium on Crows'

We convince ourselves that we have
brains so sharp we know
everything at once
and don't sort it into parts, whispered numbers

from out of date phone books
birthday cards from my dad when I was small

My ATM dispenses small bills
when you're really searching
for the million-dollar woman. Sorrow and joy
have nothing
to do with us. Meat does, and the eyes
of New Zealand spring lambs,
and rotting matter.

But I can't wait
like a lover,
wringing her hands

when all I want to do is to make a U-turn
away from the definite possibility
of simmering my love au jus
between my one size fits all thighs

Price of Gleaming

In the sun
head to heel,
bodies barred with black bands,
like seams of lead
in a church window.
Think abalone,
the wildly rainbowed
mirror of a soapbubble sphere,
think sun on gasoline.
Splendor, and splendor,
and not a one-way street,
one in any way
You are red Camaro essence. As if,
after a lifetime arriving
the jeweler's made Dollarama examples,
each as intricate
in its oily fabulation
as the one before
Suppose you could sing the ¾ bar,
like me,
would you want
to be yourself only,
unduplicatable, doomed
to be lost? Departure Bay Road
in the morning light.
Even now
you seem to be bolting
forward, add a cup of sugar honey
you won't care when we're dead
just as, presumably,
all for all,
no verb is singular,
which is the price of gleaming.

The Haunting

again and again

I couldn't waltz
with my clothes.

For naked I breathed
my first virgin breath.

Oh little green Merlin.

When you came
to my side   to my side.

Black tongues

on the edge
of the purgatorian fire

sucked the violent wet air.

We were two bloody crystals
in water's fine mist.

I ached for the secret squeeze

of your hand on mine,
leaving a haunting

of cold longing,

a spell.

If

I asked you, if I got sick and died,
would you go walking to the top of the hill

to look down on the small brown house
that we had honed from our dreams

and discontent?

Would you recall the Mexican blanket
striped with scarlet before it faded,

laid in the sun-bleached grass
you flying on top of me

gleaming with heat?

Would you hear my laugh
and feel my arms clench hard round you

guiding me to crackle and soar?

Would you remember my hand
stroking back your granite grief of loss

burrowing hope,
like a tick stuck into your still beating heart?

Would you taste
the strawberry jam I had made

hummingbird crimson
spread thinly on toast and laid at our table

sweet like our love
fierce like our sex and grid–locked complaints?

Would you hear my song like a stillborn echo
and glimpse at my chamber of remorse?

Oh, my love
would you go walking, hands swinging free
with memories of me
sloping towards my all-seeing eyes?

Otherwise

You had better believe in ghosts

Grandfather

H.W. Bilton
to Jim

My twin and I would
nestle upon his small lap. Shouting

'Tell us the one about Shadows!'

Caught up like two boats in his wave

of words, we would tremble and squeal
in anticipation of what was to come.

He painted pictures with
insinuating silence
and voices that clanged.

We would recite in thin reedy murmurs

the parts that scared us so deep,
that my grandmother would admonish
him for giving us the *Willies*.

But we would beg him

to go on
to go on

in the kerosened night.

Ten Years North

Pushing past the African plains
we doubt the dusty wizards of place.

Their fingers of heat
whisper freedom.

We leave the gray steel arrogance
ten years north

to find the sky is a watermark, bursting
into a single florid plume.

The Extravagance of Colour

The flower's stem clenched between lips
ends in a fiery open-throated bloom.

It fills the seconds with the extravagance
of red, where a song hangs lifeless

in the shattered air. She sways
with the knowledge of flame,

content to count the seconds before
its fevered tide consumes her.

The Moon

The moon is an eggshell offering,
and is above you in the pecking order.
She is the ice cream
melting in a cobalt dish.
The moon rocks the orchard
and is in your bucket twice.
She is a ventriloquist sighing
behind a mask in Venice.
She is an angler for love
and warms up her voice in the river.
The moon floods out the roads
in your head, every now and then.

New York, New York

You were ablaze
with the smear of neon
on the strip
in the hot Nevada night.

I didn't want you
to go flying, from my sight
on that hotel roller coaster
that flung you past me
and my motherly protestations.

Your face gleamed with shy appeal

so I lifted you from the trappings of safety

giving you up

to the gum-chewing kid
who measured your straight-backed desire

against the line that separated

the faint gleam of stars
and the shadowed pavement below.

You were the dangerous one
tucked under
a torn blue shirt

all ready to let go of earth
with just one step

and become part of sky.

Two Babes to Feed

You roughened the need in me
the way paper cuts skin
You silkened the need in me
the way sun melts ice
I held a need in me
and you lit it and left.
The need grew in me
till it burst into a grey canopy of ash.
The need nudged me to choose.
There was the path or the hearth
and the wind, the wind had teeth.
I stood in that wild wind, blown and undecided
and you met me with your mouth.
the wind and your mouth
roughened the need in me
and my skirts were lifted
by you and the wind.
And I chose my need for the wild,
breathe uncontained
fury of you.

One Cleft Moon

The pretty girl's neighbour drank her beauty like wine

Kept her in his breast pocket for slow days

when he danced with her silhouette
to the tune of the *Tennessee waltz*

Alone behind curtains he imagined her waist
fitting into the crux of his arm

and she whispered *bring me more than I asked for*

So he carved a cleft moon
into her bedroom door

protected her from dreams

of emerald vipers creeping
over her quivering feet

He gave her a red ribbon to tie back
the noose of her gladness

stroked her black coil of braids
that fell like a tar bridge
across their invisible fence

She danced in the twilight
with just her shimmery whimsy

so bright was her shift
of unparalleled shine

The pretty girl knew all the words to his songs

She handed him the icy flutter
of her articulated vermillion heart

Revelation flooded the rearview mirror
when he never looked back
to see

the pretty girl caught
just a one-sided poppy
stuck to a pin

How Can I Count the Stars?

I'm washed by wind, aching
for clean and cold
to wind round my thighs.

I gape with recognition

at this slack-jawed wonder
of the impossible brilliance of skin to touch.

How can I count the stars
when the dark is in the way of perfection?

Time Off

I'm free to roam
the secret landscape of my mind.

My tongue floats
in this chamber
of Jubilation

waiting to catch
the many-sided

snowflake, that is

the word.

Jude Neale is a Canadian poet, vocalist, spoken-word performer and mentor. She publishes frequently in journals, anthologies and e-zines. In international competitions, she has been shortlisted for the Gregory O'Donoghue International Poetry Prize (Ireland), the International Poetic Republic Poetry Prize (UK), the Mary Chalmers Smith Poetry Prize (UK), the Wenlock International Poetry Prize (UK), and Editor's Choice, Hurricane Press (US). She was published in A Kind of Hurricane's Best of 201/15 Anthology and was highly commended for the Sentinel Literary Quarterly Poetry Competition (UK) and for the Carers International (UK) anthology.

In Canada, Jude placed second in short story and poetry competitions run by the Royal City Literary Arts Society. Her collection *Only the Fallen Can See* was longlisted in 2012 for the Canadian ReLit Award and the Pat Lowther Award for a poetry collection by a female writer. Jude was shortlisted in the prestigious 2014 Pandora's Literary Collective Poetry Competition, achieved honourable mention in the Royal City Short Story Competition and was shortlisted twice for the Magpie Poetry Award.

A Quiet Coming of Light, A Poetic Memoir (Leaf Press, 2014), Jude's third book, was a finalist for the 2015 Pat Lowther Memorial Award, given by the League of Canadian Poets. Two of its poems were nominated for the coveted Pushcart Prize (US) by two different publishers.

One of the poems from this latest collection, *Splendid in its Silence*, was among thirty-three chosen by the 2015 Guernsey Literary Prize (UK,) to be displayed for a year on public transit in the Channel Islands. Jude was invited to read at the Guernsey Literary Festival, that year. She has also been a featured poet at The Poetry Café, Covent Garden in London.

Jude Neale
Box, 73,
Bowen Island, B.C.
V0N 1G0

judescool@hotmail.com

www.judeneale.ca